Things In Small Quantities Have Lasting Appeal

Things in Small Quantities Have Lasting Appeal

Maureen Ann Malloy

Illustrations
Liz Johnson

Academy Productions, Inc.
Cleveland, Ohio

Things in Small Quantities Have Lasting Appeal

Text: Copyright © 1996 by Maureen Ann Malloy
Illustrations and Design: Copyright © 1996 by Liz Johnson
Exclusively Published by Academy Productions, Inc.
P.O. Box 19012, Cleveland OH 44119.

Special Thanks to all my friends (especially my husband) and family members who have influenced me whether they know it or not. Also, thanks to my friends at First College, Cleveland State University, and the community of St. Mary Magdalene Parish in Willowick, Ohio.

All rights reserved. No part of this book may be reproduced or utilized in any form or by any means, electronic or mechanical, including photocopying, recording, or by any information storage and retrieval systems, without permission in writing from the publisher.

The stories contained in this collection are works of fiction. Names, characters and incidents are either the product of the author's imagination or are used fictitiously. Any resemblance to actual persons, living or dead, or events are entirely coincidental.

Library of Congress Cataloging-in-Publication Data
Things in Small Quantities Have Lasting Appeal/Maureen A. Malloy
Originally Published: Cleveland Ohio: Academy Production, Inc., 1996.
Library of Congress Catalog Card No.: 96-78847
ISBN: 0-9655355-0-9

Printed in the United States of America
by
Duke Graphics, Inc.
Eastlake, Ohio

For my parents: Marge and Jim Malloy

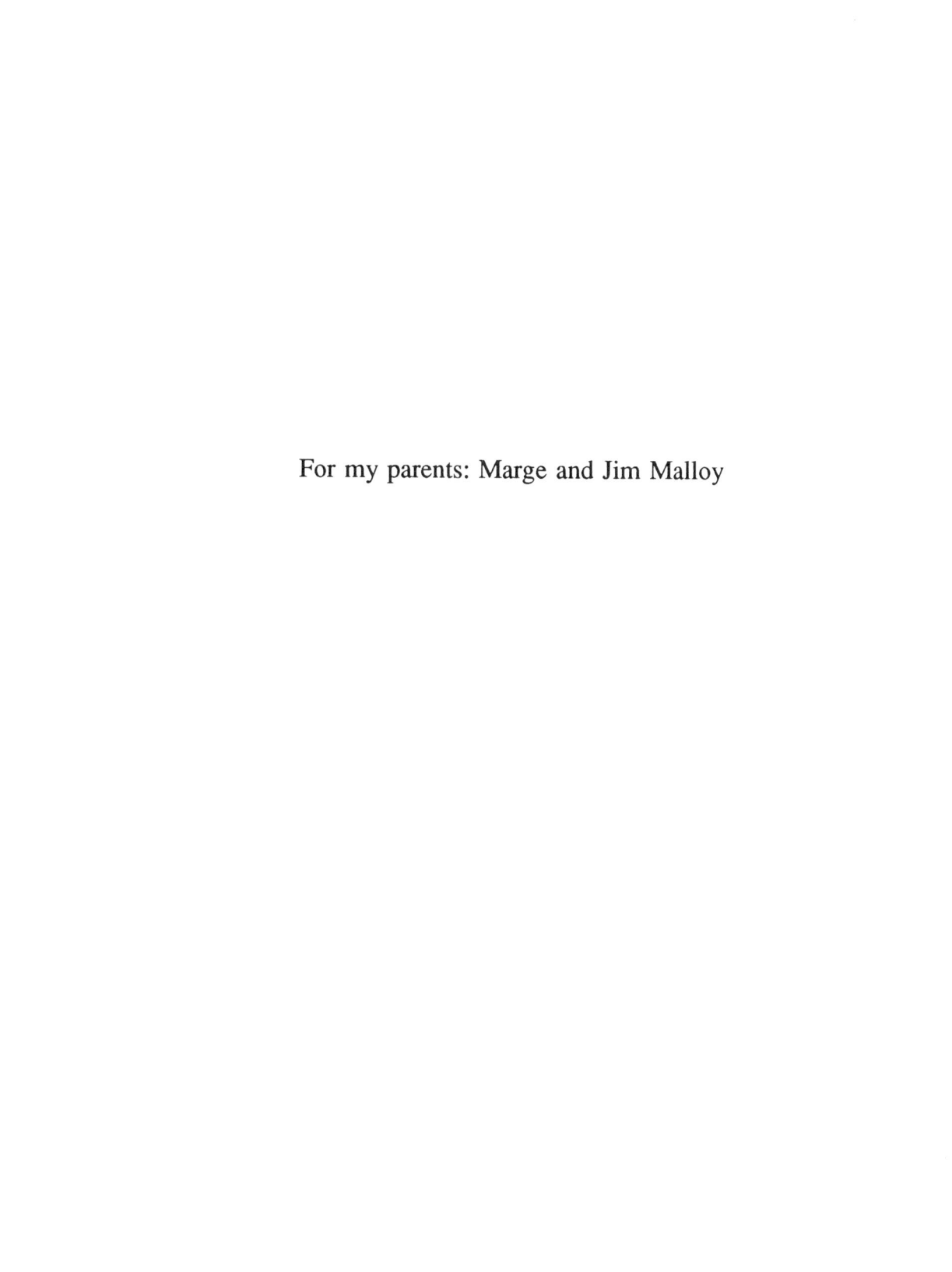

CONTENTS

One Point Of View 5

A Bed Of Leaves 9

This Life Of Storm 17

Childhood Games 21

The Navigator 35

A Couple Of Days 47

Bad News Overload (My Nightmare) 51

Lunching In The Park 56

Buddy 61

Second-Hand 70

The Church Lady 76

Stony Man 87

The Treasure 94

What I Might Say 101

Your Song 106

Strong 113

my view
is but one view

in your sight
will likely be another

the one beside you
possibly a third

and behind you
yet a fourth

possibly
a bit of truth exists
in each

Border: MICROSCOPE · PRISM · TELESCOPE · MAGNIFYING GLASS · KALEIDOSCOPE · ROSE-COLORED GLASS · KALEIDOSCOPE · MAGNIFYING GLASS · CAMERA · TELESCOPE · PRISM · MICROSCOPE · KALEIDOSCOPE · ROSE-COLORED GLASSES

One Point of View

Savannah was sitting on a folding chair on the bank of Euclid Creek when a clanking noise approached and disrupted the silence. She turned and observed a slow moving vehicle attempting to fit between two yellow strips on the pavement, somewhat similar to a child carefully shading within the boundaries of a coloring-book sketch. A grin formed on her face as she maneuvered back around and reverted to her previous activities.

Mr. Miller exited the car, now perfectly aligned in its space. He bent over, reached past the steering wheel, and pulled out two packages. He pushed down on the lock and closed the door, though leaving the window three quarters of the way open.

He came up behind Savannah. "Catch anything?" he asked.

She raised one arm, something was in her hand, and said, "Just a chapter or two." She glanced at the packages held by his side which still swayed about from the stroll up to her. "That's a big lunch," she said.

Raising the Millbrook bags slightly he responded, "For the birds." They both smiled, Mr. Miller nodded and walked away, and Savannah repositioned herself in the chair.

Another Point of View

I remember it was afternoon and my clothes kept sticking to me. It was the following day, after the funeral. Having decided I needed some distraction, I was drawn to a spot which we had so frequently found great sport. The water that day had an odor, like fish left at room temperature too long, and it looked as a framed picture with no chance of freedom from its frozen state. The surrounding melodies conspicuously lacked the rhythmical chanting of the crickets and the usual gentle encounters of the water to soil.

I heard a car pull up behind me. After turning, I discovered an older man struggling to park perfectly, not unlike my father, in a space that would take most people one try. I then directed my view again toward that book, and to that page I had been reading for the last hour.

"Catch anything?" I heard from behind me.

It was the man from the car. A reflex, casual lie blurted out, "Just a chapter or two." I really didn't feel like having a conversation with anyone, but memories of Dad flashed before me. I wondered if this man had a daughter, a wife, or maybe he was alone.

"Having lunch?" I asked as I noticed the bulging bread bags he was holding.

He smiled, "For the birds."

He raised his hand and waved, and I returned the gesture. Then, inwardly, I thanked God for my father and the time we had had together, and I blessed the old man.

A Third Point of View

> [Carol is a 54 year old housewife, president of a neighborhood watch association, and is frequently enthralled with the personal lives of her neighborhood community. She has called her husband at work (from home) as she is anxious to inform him on the latest surveyance results. Their conversation began a minute ago (past the hello).]

...and Jim, I found this journal at the lake this morning. It's incredible, shocking! I began reading it and I haven't been able to put it down since. (Pause)

I don't know, there's no name or phone number....but let me read you some, where he meets this woman. (Pause) I can tellll, the way he talks, I know it's a man. Just listen, "I discovered her in silent waiting by the river's edge on a brilliant, sun-lit day. The seagulls encircled me, as if to salute, as she laid waiting there, for years, for me. And I, the gallant warrior, Odysseus-like, returning from a great war to recapture his ever-so-loyal mistress, came to her. But like Lord Odysseus, I must perform one additional duty, but I shall return my lady and release you from your torments and fulfill your desires."

Do you believe this garbage? It's great, you've got to read it. (Pause) Ok, when you get home. Bye.

[She places the receiver down]

FREELY ALLOWING ONE'S SELF

TO

INDULGE

THE IMAGINATION

IS

TO EXPLORE

THE MIND AND SPIRIT

AND

UNVEIL A WORLD

OF

UNLIMITED

POSSIBILITIES

A Bed of Leaves

I found her on my cemented driveway, sideways, leaning on a wing,
Shivering like a pony ousting flies from the skin;
Her eyes securely shut, death hovering, she would not sing.

I thought of being late, for morning it was then, and I hesitated.
Some bread and a gift box I brought; she wanting to escape,
Her frail feet pressed against the ground, and I waited.

Mother's pouch had been declined and there she simply laid.
The work gloves were a bad idea, but I lifted her just the same,
Beside the wooden shield wall I set her, and there she stayed.

Hoping to comfort her, though knowing nature's scheme,
A bed of leaves I made for her, and I went along my way.
Returning to that place at night, the little bird no longer shook,
Quiet sadness was the scene.

PERCEPTION

IT
IS
AS
UNIQUE
AS
EACH TREE
WITHIN THE
FOREST

EACH LEAF
UPON ITS BRANCHES

AND
EACH
CREATURE
ROAMING
ITS
DOMAIN

room for thought

A goal

drives us

toward

accomplishing

much good in life

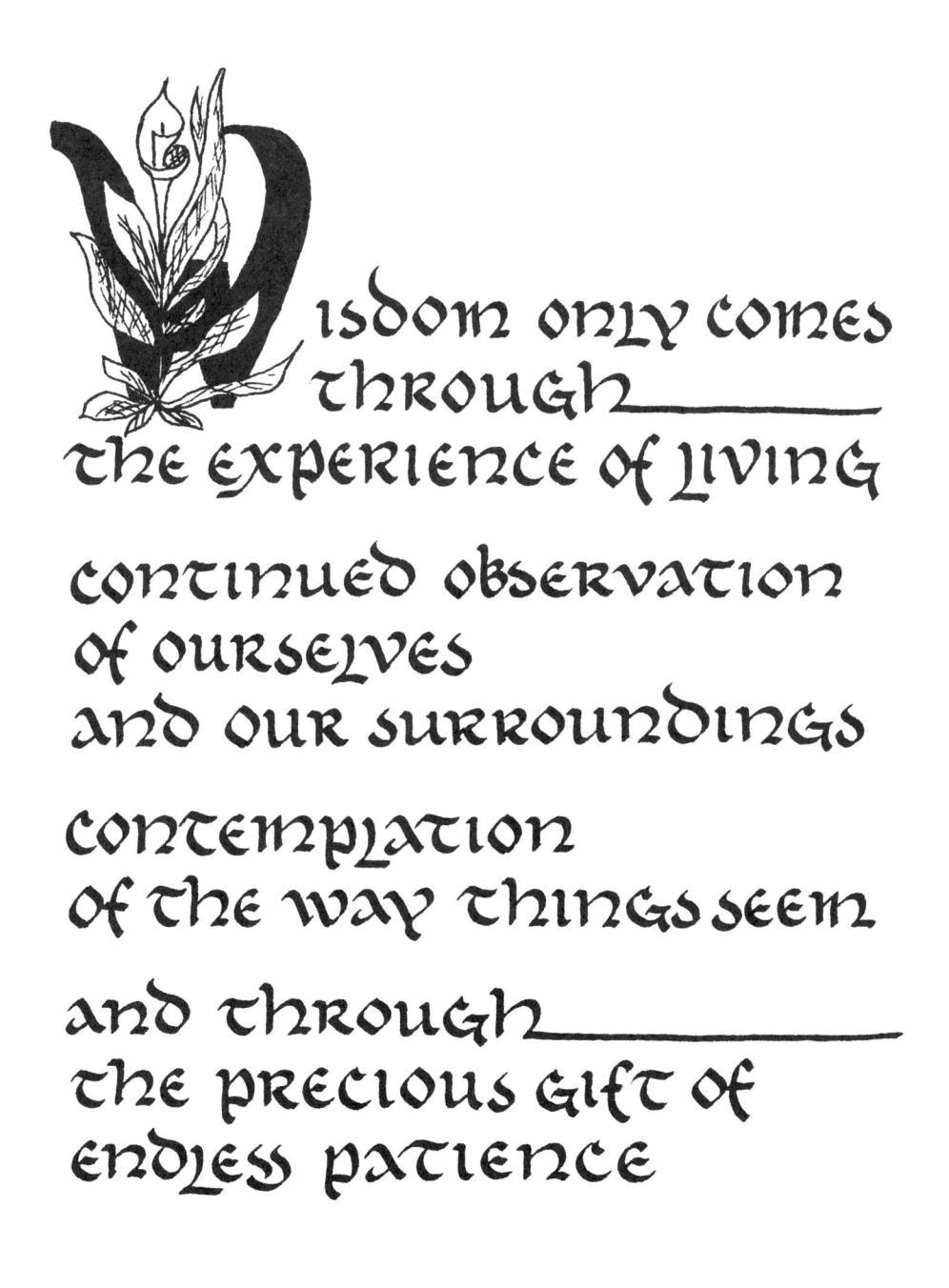

Wisdom only comes through
the experience of living

continued observation
of ourselves
and our surroundings

contemplation
of the way things seem

and through
the precious gift of
endless patience

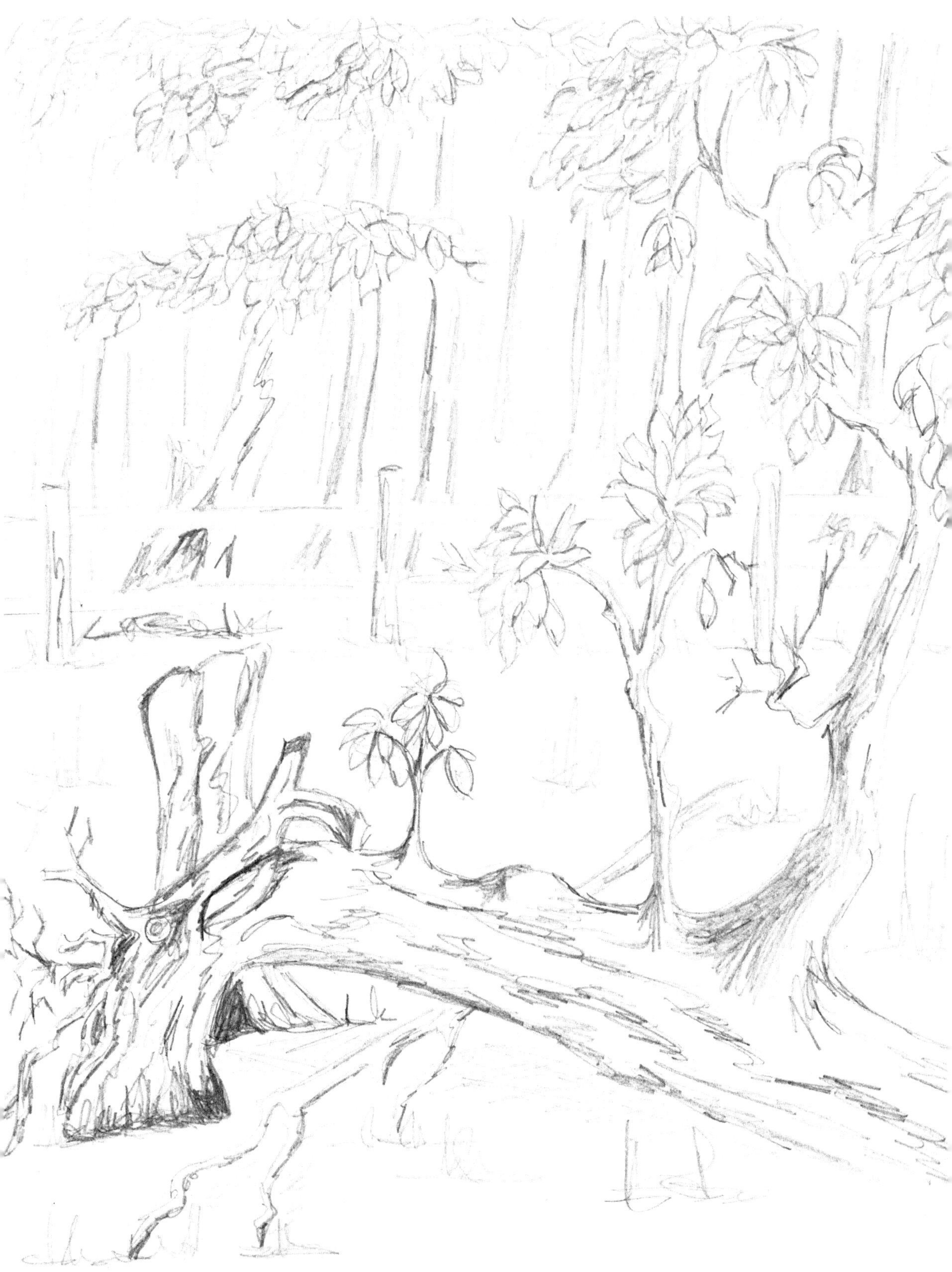

This Life of Storm

Many were the days of hot and humid conditions without the slightest hint of relief. Our local meteorologists continued issuing predictions of severe weather. But these went relatively unnoticed because the previous weeks of such prophesies had proven otherwise.

At 7:00pm, a Severe Storm Warning was issued. I was working alone that night when an emergency signal began blaring from my radio. After phoning my husband and warning him of the approaching storm, I could not resist the temptation to observe Mother-Nature in all her grand beauty and potential destructiveness.

Excitedly, I hurried to the front of the building. The only observation point was located there. I had two large windows and a door at my disposal. From the window I soon became mesmerized by a solid wall of bewitching, ominous looking clouds rolling in off the lake. Like a curtain being dropped at the abrupt conclusion of a play, day turned into night. Only the bursts of lightning illuminated the darkness now.

I could not resist the call to examine this life of storm. With wise hesitation, but driven by some unforseen force, I grasped at the imaginary barrier between us and proceeded to step through the passageway. Flying particles of dirt welcomed my entrance into its kingdom. The door was immediately torn from my grip and violently smashed against the brick building. Several times I struggled to recapture it. When finally succeeding, I pulled the door shut, using all strength that fear had bestowed.

While traveling home that evening I was showered with visions of storm. Winds had lifted whole trees from their foundations. Some were broken at their trunk and others were twisted like taffy. Trees were scattered about the parking lot, dropped across streets, and several laid upon houses throughout the neighborhood. Telephone poles had been snapped like little twigs, leaving live electrical wires to dance at your feet.

    Graceful you are,

        Dangerous you are,

            Amazing you are,

                Loved you are,

This life of storm.

We do our finest growing
while
being knocked flat
by
life's
changing
weather
patterns

IS IT ONLY
A CHILD'S
DREAM

TO BELIEVE
THAT PEOPLE
ARE
BEAUTIFUL
EXPRESSIONS OF LIFE

AND
CAPABLE
OF
UNENDING LOVE
AND
COMPASSION

CHILDHOOD GAMES

Lynne and I walked along the roadside. A dark blue van with tinted windows passed us. It slowed down and pulled off the road in front of Lynne and me; the window on the driver's side rolled down. A guy stuck his head out.

"You girls want a ride?" he asked as he held up a six pack.

Lynne laughed. "Where you going?"

"Around, the park." The man showed us the beers again.

"Sure," Lynne said and walked up to the van, not bothering to look back.

I watched her go around to the other side. The van drove away. Lynne must have gotten in because she was gone.

I stood there for a long time.

Eventually, I started walking; there were some young kids wading in the river. They splashed water back and forth until one boy jumped on top another and forced him under. Both were sopping wet when they finished struggling. Lynne and I had been friends that young. We met in Kindergarten at the public school on our street. There we learned our ABC's, met our first boyfriends, and then within a year, moved on to St. Brendan's, the gradeschool/church six blocks away.

For me, the St. Brendan years are rich with memories. Like the time we were let out early from school one Friday, for a teacher's conference, and me and Lynne had a liquid picnic in her backyard.

Lynne had filled a cooler with assorted drinks. She had them in these glass jars, like the kind my Mom used for canning jelly. The cooler was full of them. We sat on the grass in her backyard sampling each container. I didn't know, or care, what I was drinking but then neither did Lynne; she forgot what she put where. We drank, made fun of the kids at school, and stood up as soon as we had a good buzz going.

When I got home, I had trouble hiding my drunkenness, I got sick all over the bathroom floor. The next day my mother was fuming. She kept telling me, "I don't want you hanging around that girl anymore," over and over until her voice gave out. She probably kept repeating it because I wouldn't give in, I didn't say those magic words: "okay, I won't." But it just wasn't in me. I was like that with my mother anyway, always taking the opposite view and never giving in.

Lynne and I kind of got arrested once, at Gaylords. The store's been closed for years now, but back then it was one of our hangouts. It had everything in it we wanted to see, touch, try on, or steal. Gaylords was a single floor, loaded with departments kind of store. Everything you could possibly need was in it. There was a food counter by the front door which you had to walk through to get to the good stuff. Popcorn was the only decent thing they sold there. They had a clothes department, which we didn't bother with because we hated their clothes. We had to walk through it to get to the half-way-decent departments, like Records and Tapes. We spent hours upon hours there searching out our favorite bands and didn't leave until the plain clothed security guard eventually cramped our style. Gaylords had a shoe department, sports, automobile, kitchen and bathroom, and jewelry. It was in Jewelry that we had our little mishap.

"Rose, watch out for me," said Lynne when I caught up with her again.

Lynne was sticking a pair of earrings into her shirt pocket. She was very talented at this but I wished she'd given me more warning. Immediately, I scanned the area.

"Someone's coming."

Lynne and I quickly, but not exactly quietly, moved on. We knew that they couldn't touch us while we were in the store but once we're outside we'd have to watch out.

We walked out of Gaylords, the smell of popcorn ceased as the sliding glass doors shut, and Lynne pulled out a handful of jewelry.

"Here, Rose, you want some?"

"Gees, when did you pick up all that stuff?" I surveyed the handful of necklaces and earrings, which she knew I didn't wear, with the gaudy looking gold bracelet; like Elton John would wear (Lynne loved Elton John).

"I picked them up while you were in Records," she said.

"Why did you take so much stuff?"

"Just wanted to see if I could."

The next thing I heard was this guy telling us something like our rights and ushering us back inside the store. I looked at Lynne, considering making a run for it, but she didn't move, so I followed the dorky looking guy in the wrinkled blue suit (which he probably bought from Gaylords) back into the store.

They called our parents.

While we waited Lynne kept cracking jokes and laughing. It made me nervous because I thought we should at least play the part of frightened kids who were in a heap of trouble and who were going to get grounded for life, but Lynne just blew it off. For a moment our eyes met. Lynne looked scared. I was afraid for us. The guy in the wrinkled suit made us sit in his stuffy office--it had no windows or air--while he typed up some forms and added up the price tags. Nosey people kept walking in and out for a look at the day's catch. When they heard we were Catholic kids, from the school down the street, they had much more to say. They kept blaming our kleptomaniac tendencies on "those nuns." I didn't mind because it got the heat off us, but I didn't see the connection. After all, we learned to steal on our own, why should the nuns get all the credit?

When our parents came, the guy in the ugly suit told them we had been caught stealing. He claimed that Lynne had had the goods on her and that I was the lookout.

"Those gloves aren't hers either," proclaimed Lynne's mother.

"They're mine. I let her borrow them," I blurted out. The nerve of her.

In the parking lot, after being released to our parents, my parents said nothing. This was not a good sign. Normally, they had plenty to say, at least Mom did. I expected her to at least remind me that I shouldn't have been with Lynne. She had been crossed off my "allowed friends" list long ago. But she said nothing during that drive home, the longest twelve blocks in my life. Finally, we pulled into the driveway.

"I hope you're happy now," said my mother. Strangely enough, that's all she or Dad said about the episode. At least that's all I remember; I must have been grounded though, but I don't recall it. After that, I didn't go out with Lynne for a while but I saw her at school.

This must have been around seventh or eighth grade, my wild years. I did a lot of things then that I wouldn't admit, publicly anyhow.

In seventh grade, we had this woman teacher who probably shouldn't have been one because she couldn't take the stress. Mrs. McNeal was her name. Me and Lynne ended up in the same homeroom that year and we sat in the last row, ideal seats, across from each other. This one time Lynne got caught passing notes, a common crime amongst seventh graders, and Mrs. McNeal moved her desk into the cloakroom. All St. Brendan's classrooms had cloakrooms. They were actually part of the room, kind of a walk in closet where we kept our jackets and boots and stuff. They had no doors just two doorways on each side. The one in Mrs. McNeal's classroom was wide enough to fit in a student's desk. Lynne was set in there. Fortunately, she was placed just inside the opening at the back; still directly across from me, but Mrs. McNeal couldn't see her.

Lynne used to make these sounds that would really annoy Mrs. McNeal. They were like animal calls that you might hear in a jungle. Mrs. McNeal was so openly annoyed by these cackles that the whole class eventually caught on and frequently used them to tick her off. Being in the cloakroom, Lynne could more easily disguise her animal calls. Soon, we heard these low sounding but constant jungle cries. It was difficult to keep a straight face. As Lynne's noises grew louder and more frequent, the back rows began to react until the teacher could no longer ignore them. Her classroom was getting out of control and we couldn't hold back our laughter. Mrs. McNeal finally took off toward the closet. I warned Lynne with a wave of my hand and a lipped message of "she's coming." By the time the unnerved woman entered the cloakroom at the top end, Lynne had exited out the back. This went on for a while, the teacher going in one end and the student out the other. They kept missing each other. Mrs. McNeal eventually caught up with Lynne inside that room; she hollered some choice words at Lynne and made her move her desk just outside the closet where she'd be in full view.

Lynne's father had died when she was four; she told me once. Her mother was a nurse at Fairview General, but I don't have many memories of her because she wasn't around when I went over Lynne's house. Once though, her mom came over my house. She was looking for Lynne. I was on the front room floor watching the Three Stooges when she showed up. She was with Lynne's older sister (I didn't know her either).

"Have you seen Lynne, Rosemary?"

"No."

"Do you know where she is?"

"No." I wouldn't have told her anyway. The code prevented this.

"Did you talk with her today?" Her mother was staring directly at me. I could feel it.

"No." My wrist was getting sore from holding up my head but I didn't move.

"If you do, will you please call me."

"Yeah." I lied. She talked with my mother for a while, I tried to hear what they were saying, but then she and Lynne's sister left. My mother didn't say anything about that exchange to me. I wondered why but I didn't ask.

Later, after Lynne's mother had left, the phone rang. I grabbed it before it could ring a second time. It was Lynne.

"Your mom was here."

"What did she say?"

"She asked me if I saw you or knew where you were."

"What'd you tell her?"

"I told her no." I was getting worried. "What's going on, Lynne?"

She answered softly. "I ran away."

"Why?"

"Because," she said, forcing a laugh.

I watched for my parents while I waited for an answer. For a long time Lynne said nothing. I heard street sounds coming through the phone. "Where are you?"

"By Wendy's."

"Do you want me to come up?" I was worried about sneaking out of the house without being seen. If I got caught, I'd be interrogated. If I escaped, I might be followed.

"No," she said and laughed again.

I didn't know what to do. I didn't understand what she was going through. I didn't know enough, about her, about her family, her life. I tried not to cry.

"I've got to go," Lynne finally said.

"Call me if you need me, anything, okay."

"Sure, I will."

That was the last I heard from her until school started, about three weeks later. For some reason, I'm not sure why, I didn't call her house during those few weeks. When we met again in eighth grade homeroom I just said hello. She didn't seem any different. If I had known what was to come, between us, I would have said more.

This was the year, eighth grade, I got suspended off the softball team. Someone from McDonald's complained to the school that some kids from St. Brendan's caused a big scene there. The McDonald's people apparently noticed the baseball uniforms two of us were wearing. It was really nothing. After a game one Saturday, four of us shared a six pack in the park. Hardly enough to get us drunk. One of the girls looked old enough to buy beer, so we pooled our money and she bought it from a store that didn't check ID's. We sat in a clearing within the trees, in a designated drinking-smoking-whatever zone, and drank the beer.

After finishing every drop we walked under the bridge and across the railroad tracks to McDonald's. Everything was going just fine; we got in line to order and tried to be upstanding young citizens. But Lynne had other ideas. She started laughing, loudly, and dropped her french fries on the floor. She laughed even more as she swayed and tripped her way up to get another fry. It was a classic case of over-acting, but funny; Lynne was always funny. We ate there, joked around, and then left.

Monday morning, when the announcements came over the loud speaker, we were informed that the girl's softball team must meet after school. I had a bad feeling about this. We met in a second floor classroom. The principal came in first, followed by our coaches.

"I want to know which of you girls went to McDonald's after the game Saturday. All games will be canceled until I find out," and then she walked out, with the coaches, and shut the door. Just like that.

It was odd that she didn't give anyone a chance to respond, not that anyone would, but she just left. I looked out the window. The hundred-year-old school guard, Charlie, was stopping traffic again. He held the cars back while a few young stragglers crossed the street. A lot of chattering was going on in the room.

The principal came back in.

"So, which of you was at McDonald's Saturday?"

Me and another girl raised our hands. Then, there was this long discussion about whether the whole team should be punished (for our crimes). I listened. The principal, coaches, and the team eventually decided to suspend me and the other girl. We couldn't play for the next five games. There were only six left in the season. Anyhow, a few days later, the principal drove the now famous four to McDonald's where we had to apologize and order a small fry with a small pop like young ladies. You'd think they'd spring for a Large, considering the humiliation we had to go through. Lynne was with us; I didn't know how she got caught because she wasn't on the team.

Lynne and I had been attending the same high school before she got into that van.

We were teenagers. Lynne and me had taken a bus to the entrance of the park, right by Fairview Hospital. We walked down the steep, winding path into the valley. The valley was this huge park system where people had picnics, walked, road bikes, played ball, waxed cars, and cruised around looking for girls and guys. There were dozens of hiking trails which either cut into the woods or followed along the fast flowing and sometimes over flowing Rocky River; the scenery was beautiful.

Lynne and I walked along the roadside. These jerks in cars kept honking their horns at us. Lynne waved her standard gestures back and yelled other colorful remarks. A dark blue van with tinted windows passed us several times; its windows were the kind not sold anymore because they've been outlawed. The van pulled off the road just in front of us. The window on the driver's side began rolling down. An older guy in his late twenties stuck his head out. He had a partially grown in beard and long, black and greasy hair; he was holding a Miller Light.

"You girls want a ride?" he asked while holding up a string of four beers left from a six pack.

Lynne laughed. She didn't look at me. "Where you going?" Lynne asked and laughed again. She swayed her body back and forth as if she were drunk.

"Around, the park." The man held up the beers once more.

"To park." She laughed. "Sure," she said and walked over to the van, not even hesitating.

I watched her walk around to the other side. I wondered if anyone was inside looking out of those windows. The van drove away. Lynne must have gotten in because she was gone.

A couple weeks later, I saw Lynne while riding my bike home from soccer practice. She was across the street. I thought about going up to her but she looked different. I just kept riding and pretended not to see her; she probably did the same.

After that day, I saw Lynne occasionally at school. I avoided her. Once she got expelled and then moved away, it became much easier. Years later, I saw her at a grade-school reunion. She had put on a lot of weight and was still laughing at everything. The laughing would have been great if I thought it was real.

I haven't seen her since.

Life is a teeter-totter

that's rarely
in balance

Some big kid keeps getting on the other side
and tossing me into the air

Then he jumps off without warning me
and I crash
to the ground

My feet hurt
My back hurts
My butt hurts

This game is rough

I keep looking for some kid my size
to balance this thing

Sometimes I find one
and
I
take
a
breather

Look in the mirror

into
your eyes

and
say

I love you

then
look into the eyes of another
and say
the same

The Navigator

BRIDGE CLOSED FOR REPAIR

The Navigator

I am the NAVIGATOR. It is my job to find the way. But state maps don't include back roads! However, I think we're going East, so eventually we'll either hit our destination, or a main route, or maybe some farmer who could give us directions.

Our search is for a small town in Pennsylvania known as Wyalusing. We are traveling along a wide, rapidly flowing river, to which according to the map, the town is adjacent. We should be arriving at a bridge very soon.

A grayish, steel bridge appears in the distance, about half a mile ahead (being Navigator I can judge these things). As we approach it, we see a train track hugging the river and a few small houses scattered along the water's edge. Surely, this must be Wyalusing.

Upon finally reaching the bridge we are met by a sign. It has large white letters which read "Wyalusing" and an arrow pointing directly across the river. Unfortunately, there is another larger, brighter, meaner and nastier sign saying:

"Bridge Closed for Repair."

Interestingly enough, it is closing for 30 days and today is day 1 of 30.

It gets better.

There is this construction worker. He has a yellow hard hat resting on his head, heavy work boots guarding his feet, and dirt covered clothes covering his body. We ask this friendly looking gentlemen, "How do we get to Wyalusing from here?"

He begins to laugh. You know the kind of laugh that screams out a person's real thoughts. I clearly hear him thinking:

"You're really far off the beaten path."

"You'll never find it."

"You're not from around these parts."

He finally manages to compose himself again and says, "Ya go back about 25 miles, when you run across a church, make a left, then you go about another few miles till ya hit Tug's Tavern, make a left, keep going until ya hit Wyalusing."

We didn't find it.

I, the Navigator, a little bruised from failure, located another town (on this side of the river) and reached it with NO problem (that I remember).

Don't you just love being NAVIGATOR?

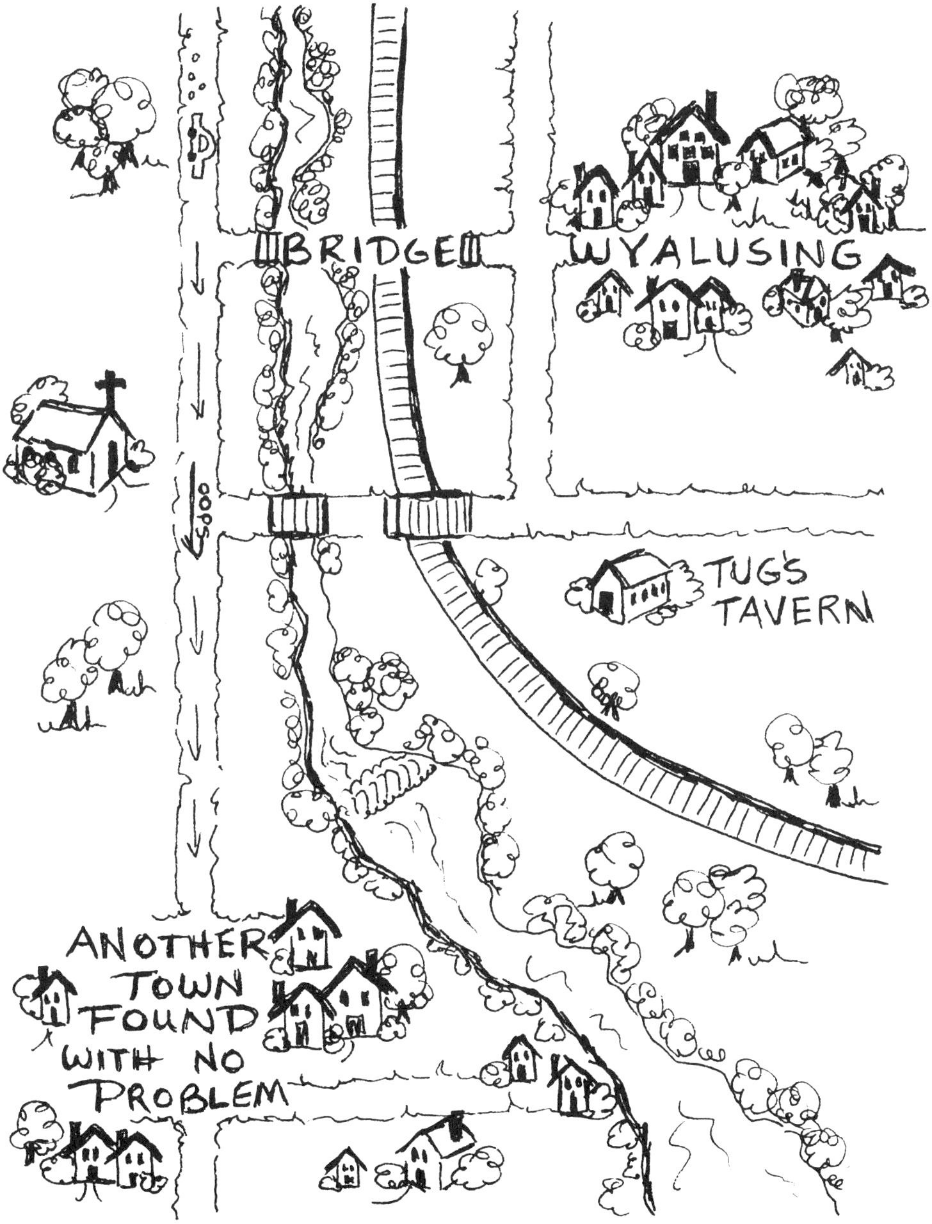
BRIDGE
WYALUSING
OOPS
TUG'S
TAVERN
ANOTHER
TOWN
FOUND
WITH NO
PROBLEM

I went fishing the other day with my new rod.
(That's what they call it. Right?)

I caught the BIGGEST FISH I'VE EVER SEEN!
ANYwhere!
REALLLY!
(At least on my line.)

It was a twelve-and-a-half inch largemouth bass.
(That's what they told me.)

I only screamed and yelled a little when I pulled—
No, REELED it in.
(Nobody complained.)

I had to take it off the line.
I had to touch it
I didn't flinch.
(If someone'd offered, I'd let them help.)

I like parts of fishing.
(Some parts I don't.)

When you find your river and carefully examine it it will lead you to your ocean of potential

STEPPING OUT OVER THE CLIFF AND INTO YOUR FEARS IS EXTREMELY FREEING

flying is discovering
truths
about yourself
and your reality

freedom
becomes your companion
and
the spirit of life
serves as your guide

room for thought

A COUPLE OF DAYS

The Village People are singing "Macho, Macho Man...," it's disco night on 104FM. Her monitor screen is completely blue, except for the current date and a bright blinking cursor sustaining a fixed, unwavering rhythm. Though rather an ancient computer, and second-hand at that, it performs word processing well enough.

She studies over some scribbling in her journal. A dictionary, with its binding severely bent, is stationed upon the diskette holder. Her book of words is always present when she strikes the keys. Without it, she becomes as a child lacking its most cherished nap blanket and she cannot slumber until its return. Glancing up at the screen and involuntarily squinting, Ann angles the monitor away from the lamp light's reflective glare. She returns to her notes.

Moving the kitchen chair back from the front room desk, she shifts her body to the right, toward the phone on the floor and the radio up top (now playing KC and the Sunshine Band). She bends over, rests her elbows on her thighs, and positions her hands on her face, just below the cheek bones. Ann stares at her feet.

"My socks are so white."

Ann removes the lopsided earphones, which afford sound from the left side only, withdraws the cord from the radio, a 22nd birthday present from ten years ago that is yet missing its antenna, and lays it upon the table. She stands up, adjusts her faded blue sweat pants, and walks into the dining room, past her husband playing cards on the floor. They exchange no words. Moving into the kitchen, she reaches for the designated water cup, turns on the cold water, fills the see-through Tupperware glass approximately one-quarter full and drinks it down.

She leaves the kitchen, steps by her husband again, with his head directed downward engrossed in his own version of Solitaire, and grabs a healthy bunch of his unruly hair. Ann yanks slightly. She observes a grunting noise emerge from the immobile one and a grin escapes her features. Continuing into the front room, she settles again in the chair. Her fingers now perched on the keyboard, she begins to write.

Several hours later she says, "Hey, Tom, you wanna hear it?" "Sure," he responds and rises. He enters the room, and plots himself down on the couch. Ann looks at him across the room. "It's really, really, really rough, but tell me what you think." She focuses her eyes again on the word-cloaked screen and begins to recite, consciously resisting an ever present urge to clarify its content. They discuss it briefly, include praise and opportunities for enhancement, and retire to the kitchen to fix a double-batch of well-buttered, overly salted popcorn.

It's late now, so Ann and her husband go to bed.

After gobbling some morning toast and juice, she kisses Tom good-bye. Not so much later she commences the routine.

One hand clinches the wooden mantel above the fireplace as she casually balances herself on the rear legs of the seat. She often follows this custom while proof-reading a piece. Allowing the armless chair to reestablish its intimate relationship with the carpet, she begins to revise. Interrupted only by an itch, she maneuvers her hand beneath the sleeve of her T-shirt and scratches unconsciously until relief.

"can I help?"

The most frightening
three words
in our vocabulary

Not to worry though

The
real challenge
only comes
when someone responds

YES!

IN
DARKNESS
I
SEE

CLEARER

Bad News Overload (My Nightmare)

I opened my eyes, though quite unsure of reality, I became aware that my heart was beating far beyond its norm, tears were streaming down my face, and my hands were clinched beneath the blankets.

I rarely remember my dreams, but when I do, not much detail is provided. However, this one was clearly and freshly planted in my mind. It was one of those dreams that you spontaneously awaken from when you can no longer bear the situation your in.

Once sure of my awakened state, I reached for my husband, hugged him closely, and whispered to him my fears. Then I proceeded to describe my nightmare.

It was at the old house, in the place where I grew up, the house that my parents just sold last year.

It was summertime when I walked into that vacant house. People began appearing and disappearing without warning. At first, I recognized no one and I thought they were robbing the place. I remember thinking they were bikers, but later I determined they were friends of a relative who had previously fallen from grace.

Next, I was sitting by the window in the dining room when a nasty looking storm began to roll in. Strange people became visible and joined me in the room (they turned out to be reporters).

My mind must have wandered again as it decided to change the scene. Summer became winter and a charmingly decorated Christmas tree appeared. The thunderstorm transformed into a blizzard and I found myself explaining our Christmas tree decorating techniques to the news media.

Then I was beamed upstairs into one of the back bedrooms. It looked just like it had when it was my room (after most of my brothers and sisters moved out). I saw my reflection in the dresser mirror.

Summer had again returned and a crack of thunder rumbled outside my window. The thunder then became a bomb blast and shook the house from roof to basement. Gun-fire then began and a mini-war broke out around me. I dropped to the floor.

At that very moment, my sister appeared and I yelled at her to "Get Down!" (she seemed oblivious to the machine-gun fire). I pulled her safely to the ground.

Next, my sister rudely vanished (as my bizarre mind so instructed) and I started crawling down the stairs. It was then I realized that the gunfire was coming from downstairs (in the house). The gunfire became so loud and clear that I realized I was caught in the cross-fire. I took cover on the stairs and waited for it to pass.

Then it stopped. I cautiously arose from the stairway to find my mother and father in the living room. They were acting as if nothing had happened. Mom was on a footstool, which I did not recognize, and she was arranging her Hummel display. Dad was sitting on the couch reading his newspaper.

I told Mom to "Get Down!" (after all this was a War-Zone). Then I noticed a sharp-shooter pointing a gun into the window. I looked back at my mother and somehow the footstool and her miraculously shot across the room out of gun-range. Then I discovered that the gunman was my brother and he was outside safe-guarding the house.

The scene that followed placed me outside with my father and I was feeling rather shaken from the day's events. He seemed light-hearted and casual while he jokingly referred to a potential drive-by-shooting. This was t-o-o weird.

Next, four cars collided a few houses down the street. A woman opened her car door and began screaming. A bundle was thrown from her grip during the accident, this was her focus and concern. Just then, another automobile came racing down the street and the woman screamed at it to stop. Someone even rammed a car into the speeder's but this failed to alter its course. I heard the sound of crushing bones beneath its wheels.

At that moment I realized that the bundle was a child. I dropped to my knees, broke into tears, and covered my face with my hands in disbelief and sorrow.

I immediately awoke.

You know, I think my husband's right, I watch too much news.

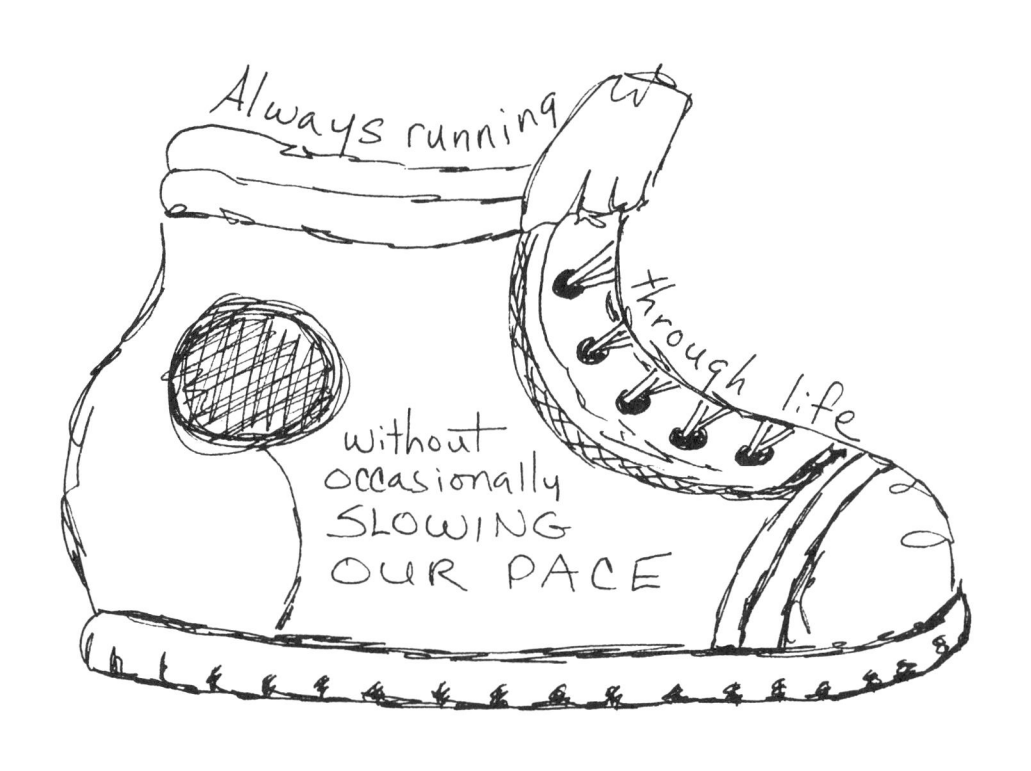

Always running through life without occasionally SLOWING OUR PACE

can lead to bad knees

LUNCHING IN THE PARK

Today the snow is steadily falling and the road is barely visible. If I didn't know the way, a ditch would be a likely place to find me.

The parking lot is empty now except for a few brave souls. I leave the car running to prevent a case of frostbite. Lunch is devoured rapidly while the windshield wipers struggle to clear my view.

The trees are nearly leafless now, but the freshly fallen snow eagerly clings to their branches. An impenetrable, eerie silence has all life appearing suspended. Only my soul detects the life.

In the winter months, I do most of my reading here. It seems only appropriate since the warm months are filled with much activity. People watching is at its peak and nature walking is a must.

But it is winter now and a good novel is beckoning; or maybe not such a good novel.

Lunch hour passes quickly and it is time to return. Farewell to this vision of inspiring peacefulness. I go again into a reality of pressure and calamity. Though once removed from sight, this knowledge I will take...

When sadness or madness
    encompasses the mind
        and
  perspective calls my name
this scene of beauty shall be revisited
        and
      peace
    will fill my heart

LIFE
IS LIKE
A BANANA

if you don't eat it up
it
will

ROT

IT CAN TAKE YEARS TO DISASSEMBLE A WALL BUT ONLY SECONDS TO REBUILD IT

BUDDY

With the last load of laundry sorted and filed away, Sandy decides to get the mail. It's two o'clock and it's usually here by now. Sandy unlocks the screen door latch, jiggles it--it's stuck again--and pushes the door aside; it swings shut behind her. The mailbox is on the tree lawn, as are all the other mailboxes on the street. Sandy must walk to the curb to get it. As she reaches the third step off the porch, the pest strikes. It charges, only the thumping of its feet against the grass provide her with any warning. Sandy jumps back and screams, but the pest stops just short of her, five feet no less, as it's jolted backwards by the chain around its thick neck.

"My God, don't do that," she breathes out seeing her assailant firmly tied to her neighbor's post. "Stop doing that, I mean it dog." The ambusher peers back at Sandy, pulling tightly on its restraints, and barking savagely. Sandy grabs her mail and hurries back into the house, keeping one eye on that chain.

Several weeks later, Sandy is putting her soiled hiking boot into hot rushing water. She quickly draws back her hand, having received an unplanned and unpleasant shower.

"I hate that dog, it's gonna be me or that dog. Stupid mut."

She grabs a paint mixer from inside the Folger's coffee can; it's thin and wooden and looks like a ruler without the markings. With the mixer, she scrapes off the thick, stubborn brown-stuff between the deeper grooves. She back-steps away from the stink and shuts her eyes, trying hard to avoid any thoughts of lunch. Having regained her composure, Sandy continues the unfortunate task.

Twenty minutes later she hears the side door slam. Her husband is calling down to her but Sandy can't make out what he's saying over the high-pitched hum of the running water. He walks partially down the steps.

"Sandy, watcha doing?"

"I'm cleaning dog shit off my new shoes." Sandy yells toward the steps.

"Breaking them in already?"

Sandy looks up. "I'm telling you, it's either me or that dog. We're gonna have it out, and only one of us will walk away." She pokes harder and faster into the grooves, wanting to remove every spec.

"It's the owner you should be mad at."

"Yah, but I can't kill the owner, so it'll have to be the dog." Sandy continues her work.

Returning from Kmart, she now has the required materials: a pack of large black letters, a dog whistle for emergencies, two sticks of wood for the backing and a stand, two Snickers bars, and a twelve ounce bottle of rat poison.

"You sure you want to do this?" asks her husband.

"Yes, I'm gonna fix that mut and Mrs. Levy too." At the side door, Sandy hands him one of the candy bar's, steps by him, and skips directly down into the basement. She chucks the bag of necessary equipment onto the workbench, takes a hammer from the left drawer, and immediately begins. Her husband disappears somewhere, but downstairs the happy worker is lining up stickers to form two words. She chuckles while considering what she'd much rather spell out: "No %@^$#%*&^ Dogs!, No Stupid Fool's Muts!, All Dogs and Owners Will Be Shot On Sight!, You Trespass, You Die!"

The neighbor's side door shuts, Mrs. Levy's door, and two old woman's legs appear outside the window. Tapping sounds come from the four legged beast beside her; it's jumping about as if it's just been unshackled. Mrs. Levy has been Sandy's neighbor for fourteen years now and only recently, last year that is, has she lived alone. Her children have all married and moved away. The nearest lives on Bennington Street - which is actually only a few blocks away, but she wanted a constant companion. So she bought Buddy. He's a mix between an Alaskan

Husky and a Wolf. He has deep blue eyes that make you wonder what force exists behind them. Buddy has lots of energy. When Mrs. Levy lets him roam around the backyard, he runs inside the fence barriers and chases squirrels, birds, cats, and anything else that mistakenly enters his territory. He barks a lot too.

Mrs. Levy takes her dog for a walk every evening, but mostly after sunset, so he can do his business on other peoples' lawns. She apparently doesn't want her yard diminished by the taint of animal waste. After all, she spends so much time and effort caring for her flowers and her garden and her lawn. Most of the people in the neighborhood don't care anything about their yards since they never work on them. Only a few neighbors make any effort to plant flowers, trim bushes, pull weeds, or even properly mow their lawns. They probably don't even notice Buddy's little droppings.

"There, it's finished." Sandy holds her creation up and broadly smiles. She parades upstairs, remembering to bring the hammer, and walks into the kitchen to show her husband the finished product. "So, what do you think?"

"NO DOGS!", he reads. "Very nice, very direct, I like it."

"I'm gonna put it out there now. I would just die to see Mrs. Levy's face when she reads it."

Outside, she stops in the driveway until her eyes adjust to the darkness. Then she marches onto the front lawn. The hairy mongrel and its owner are a dozen houses down the street; still out on their nightly raid. After carefully directing her "No Dogs!" decree toward Mrs. Levy's house, she hammer's it into the ground. A street light is perfectly located in front of Mrs. Levy's house which kindly illuminates the sign; they can't possibly miss it.

Sandy takes one last look down the street in hopes of seeing them. Unfortunately, they're not in sight. She feels a bit let down, having gone to all this trouble, and thinks the least they could do is show up; but she goes back inside to wait.

Sandy plops down on the front room sofa but is hardly able to remain still. She shoves the curtain aside and peeks out the window. Nothing. The television is on, her husband's watching something, so she watches too. Every few minutes she checks the yard for movement.

A while after her husband had gone to bed, Sandy probes the lawn once more. "Where could they be?" She finally goes to bed.

It's nine-twenty, Wednesday morning and Sandy has forgotten to set out the trash, or that is, to remind her husband to; the garbagemen always pickup before eleven and sometimes earlier. The sky is clear, the sun is bright, and the rather fine assortment of neighborhood birds is awake and singing. Sparrows, finches, doves, robins, and, unfortunately, some pigeons are gathered around the backyard feeder. Many are standing on the ground, gobbling up the dropped seeds from the sloppier eaters, and some wait patiently on branches within the tree for their turn upon the food dispenser.

A slight breeze greets Sandy as she opens the back door and moves onto the porch. She's wearing her new boots. She's holding a Hefty bag. The garbage cans are behind the garage; right next to the fence which divides the properties. She lugs the trash bag back behind the garage, lifts up the lid, and drops the package inside. Savage barking and the charging hound make her drop the lid and it crashes to the ground.

"Oh, shit." She exhales. "Oh my God, it's you, you scared the living shit out of me, you mangy mut." Sandy recognizes its wishful stare as the gate between them prevents its further advancement.

"Now Buddy, what are you playing with?" Mrs. Levy calls out from her kitchen window.

Sandy begins dragging the two garbage cans out front. "It's just me Mrs. Levy." She adds in a low mumble, "He's just playing with me, that oversized-stalking-furball."

"Hello there, Sandy. You better hurry up or you'll miss the pickup, and it'll get awfully stinky back there. My beautiful flowers wouldn't like that at all."

Sandy mumbles again and the dog follows along the fence. It watches her constantly until she moves beyond its sight; she leaves the pest behind sniffing in the air. The hairy nuisance must wait. Continuing her descent toward the street, she pulls the load past the weather-worn back porch, past the green tangled hose against the house, past the front porch, and beside the lawn which had held her interest so long the night before.

"My sign." She turns toward Mrs. Levy's house wondering if the old woman had the gall to steal it. Only a few splinters remain in the ground where it was proudly mounted just hours before. After placing the remaining shreds into the trash can, she yanks the garbage to the curb. She brushes her dirt covered hands together and walks back.

Returning through the backyard gate, she finds the dog there still guarding his post and gazing her way. Aware of its heavy breathing like a bull before the charge, she stops at the bottom step and turns. Their eyes meet. She cannot resist the urge; she swings her arms and stamps her feet and the beast charges, smashing his face against the fence that he's forgotten is there.

"Ha, got you. Stupid mut." She walks inside laughing though still upset about her stolen sign (not yet having noticed the fresh deposit on her boots). Sandy wonders what the dog would do if ever it caught her alone, minus the fence between.

It's mid-afternoon and Mrs. Levy has gathered a fine pile of stray leaves and sticks in her backyard. Buddy sniffs it thoroughly. The unwelcome collection has come, she thinks, from Sandy's tree or possibly from another neighbor's tree, but mostly from Sandy's tree. Knowing this, Mrs. Levy decides to return her neighbor's property. She clutches a handful of debris, looks around, creeps up to the fence, and drops it into Sandy's yard. She goes back for more and tosses another handful over, trying to spread it around. During the fifth trip, her shirt gets caught on the fence after leaning forward too much; she was hoping for good distance. Instead, she's stuck, standing on her tiptoes, and practically hanging from the fence.

Sandy's reading a book, "Dogs That Don't Fetch," when she hears barking. It's pitch is lower than normal and it's rhythm seems sporadic and playful. Usually, only two kinds of barks come from that direction. The first is an "I want to eat you bark" and it's very rapid and high pitched. The second is a steady, consistent, annoying, and rhythmic type of barking which goes on for hours. This bark is different, though it is coming from Mrs. Levy's backyard. After ten minutes it becomes distracting as Sandy has read the same paragraph several times.

From Sandy's back porch, she hears barking but she cannot see the loudmouth itself. "What is your problem?" The noise continues. Sandy walks toward the neighbor's yard, following the commotion, and sees the dog first. It's standing there howling at Mrs. Levy who appears to be climbing over the fence. She moves around behind the garage to get a closer look and finds Mrs. Levy tugging at her shirt.

"Mrs. Levy, are you alright?"

"No. I'm not alright, your fence attacked me."

Sandy trudges through some leaves to get to her. It's difficult to lift her enough to unhook the shirt; she's got all her weight on it. "I can't seem to get leverage, I'll have to come around."

"Well then, hurry up. I'm beginning to sprout buds." Sandy runs around to Mrs. Levy's gate but the dog is there.

He looks.

She looks.

Neither moves. She finally places her hand on the latch and he growls; the hair on his back rises to attention. She stops. He waits.

She slowly unlatches the lock and he lifts his front legs as if adjusting his weight; the gate is now unlocked though still closed. Sandy carefully pushes the gate aside, keeping a firm grip just in case, until it's fully open with no obstruction remaining between. "Nice doggy, pretty doggy, don't bite me doggy," she says in a kind of baby-talk voice, hoping to charm the beast. As she takes one smooth step forward the gate keeper shifts toward her. Sandy halts and wonders how she got herself into this predicament; remembering teasing the dog earlier and how really ticked off it had been. Hearing Mrs. Levy again shaking the fence about persuades her to continue. Cautiously, she maneuvers herself around the dog while keeping constant eye-contact with it. Buddy follows her all the way back to where Mrs. Levy is hanging.

It doesn't take Sandy too long to release Mrs. Levy from the fence's clutches, but she's quite ruffled. Sandy brings her some pink lemonade and sits on her porch steps with her until she calms down. Just inside the screen door, Sandy notices a sign leaning against Mrs. Levy's pantry wall. She let's it go for now.

The dog is watching Sandy. Sandy wants to leave and hopes to get back onto her side of the fence. The dog moves in closer. It sniffs her feet. She worries about the potential problems if it should recognize her scent. The forgetful dog barks.

"Oh now Buddy, this is our neighbor, Sandy. So you be nice." With much urging from Mrs. Levy, she reluctantly extends her hand in friendship toward Buddy. "This way he'll get your scent." Sandy doesn't want that.

A few hours later, Sandy returns from Urgent Care; the doctor has told her the stitches will come out in two weeks.

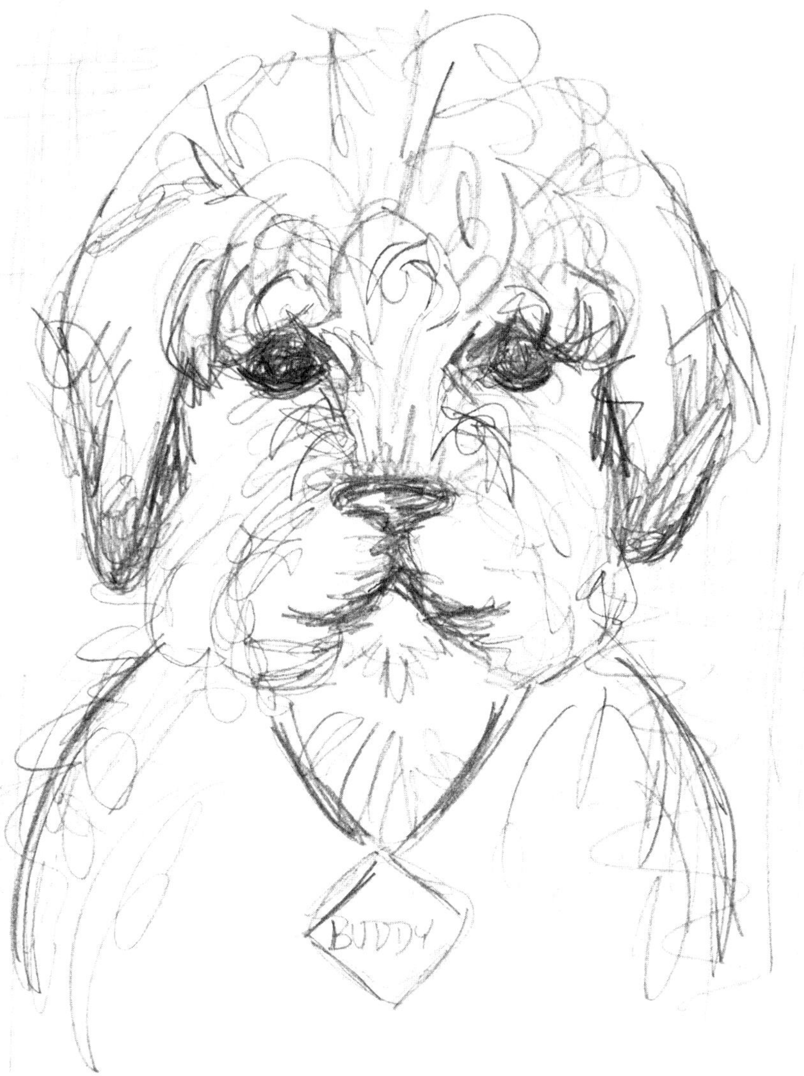
BUDDY

"Never take yourself too seriously

'CAUSE NOBODY ELSE DOES"

SECOND-HAND

CHARACTERS
Mike (The husband)
Susan (The wife)

SETTING
Living room of the couple's house. House is simply furnished. Includes a sofa, two lamps (one lamp-shade is worn, it has holes), two end tables, duck wall paintings, a phone, a small bookcase, and an old fireplace (no longer in use).

At curtain, Mike is on one knee. He is carefully setting up a second-hand fireplace set which is severely tarnished from age. After a moment, Susan walks into the room and notices him arranging it.

SUSAN: You're kidding, right?

MIKE: (He stands up and looks her way.) Whaaat?

SUSAN: You're not putting it there!

MIKE: Ooohhh..Yes I am! Where else would you put a fireplace set?

SUSAN: How about the garage, where no one can see it.

MIKE: (He turns his head toward the fireplace.) Well, I like it! It looks nice in front of the fireplace. Besides, your mother gave it to us.

SUSAN: (She walks toward it.) Soooo. It looks stupid! It's older than I am. It doesn't match anything in here, and she won't remember who she gave it to anyway.

MIKE: (Blocking Susan from reaching the set.) Now, don't you touch it!

SUSAN: C'mon, I'll put it somewhere where we can both appreciate it.

MIKE: Like where?

SUSAN: Like, GoodWill!

MIKE: No, no. I don't think so.

SUSAN: (She cuddles up to him.) Ah, c'mon honey, sweetie. Don't you love me anymore?

MIKE: (He smiles.) Yes.

SUSAN: Don't you want to please me in every possible way?

MIKE: Yes.

SUSAN: (She lurches toward the fireplace.) Well then, let me have that ugly thing!

MIKE: (He holds her back again.) No. You can't have it!

Get away!

SUSAN: (She turns away from him, feeling discouraged.) Fine. I'll just wait till you're not home. Then I'll bury it in the backyard with the dog shit.

MIKE: You wouldn't do that.

SUSAN: Yes I would. And you know it.

MIKE: You're right. I do.

SUSAN: So why don't you save yourself the trouble and shock, and let me take it now.

MIKE: No. Besides, I hardly have anything in here I really want.

SUSAN: Oh really. How about those billions of "How To books" clogging up our bookcase.

MIKE: You took most of them out when you were rearranging it! (He points to a pile of books in the corner.) They're all over here, on the floor.

SUSAN: Oh. (Pause. She walks toward some framed paintings on the wall, then points to them.) How about these pathetic duck paintings all over the wall. I hate ducks! I've always

	hated ducks! Why do people always give us presents with ducks on em? We've got duck kitchen towels, duck bathroom towels, duck cups, duck cards, and stupid duck figurines. I hate ducks!!
MIKE:	So what's your point.
SUSAN:	That issss my point.
MIKE:	So take down the ducks. I'll keep my fireplace set.
SUSAN:	I don't want to take down the ducks. I want to take down that!
MIKE:	No.
SUSAN:	Now you're ticking me off. (Pause.) Look, I'll trade you something for it.
MIKE:	(A hopeful smirk forms on his face.) Oooo...Whatcha got in mind, baby?
SUSAN:	No. Not that, PERVERT! How about...I'll buy you a lamp-shade. (She gestures at the timeworn lamp.) You've always wanted one without holes. We can go get one. Right now!
MIKE:	I like this one. It adds character to the place.

SUSAN: C'mon, Mike, I really hate that thing. (Pause.) It holds bad memories for me.

MIKE: Oh yah, Like What?

SUSAN: My mother used to chase me around...with the poker.

MIKE: Nice try.

SUSAN: No. No. Really. Let me have it. I'll give it to one of my brothers or sisters.

MIKE: (The phone rings and he walks toward it.) Alright, alright. If you hate it that much... (He picks up the receiver.) Hello...well hellooo!...why yes, she's right here. Oh, Suuusan, it's your mooother.

SUSAN: (She slowly trudges to the phone. Mike hands it to her.) Hi, mom...Yes, it's lovely...it looks wonderful in our living room...I love you too mom, bye.

MIKE: (He looks at her with a hesitant grin.)

SUSAN: I hate you. (She stomps out of the room.)

MIKE: Yes dear.

(Curtain)

TAKING PEOPLE
AS THEY ARE
IS
LESS
AGGRAVATING

THE CHURCH LADY

She sits alone in chosen isolation. Her head is sloped forward, but her owl eyes remain alert; her hands are folded on her lap. The slightly wrinkled dress she wears reeks of incense. This and the past several weekends, in that same pew, Mrs. Cumberlan secretly observes the activities of her attention. She writes notations in a palm-size notebook that she conceals within the right pocket of her polyester-cotton sweater. Then, like a hawk's triumphant flight after snatching a mouse from a field, she rises and swiftly moves toward the exit.

At the house, a neighbor gathering leaves pauses and looks her way, she focuses forward and scurries up the driveway. The woman on a mission opens the side-door and steps in, unconsciously removing her shoes and leaving them by the mat. She takes the journal from her pocket, lays it on the kitchen table next to some old photos, and opens it. Two hours later, she snatches the top book from a paper bag full of bounded works and tears out a single, somewhat blank page. She begins to write:

Candy Cotleur (best now)
Kevin Lander (director)
Sue Lander (his wife)...

Thursday arrives and she slowly draws back the door at St. Anthony's. She hovers by the entrance awhile, considering the assemblage, although inside it's rather dim as only a few lights are illuminating. The members are scattered before the sanctuary and are engaged in several, private conversations. Eventually, the unidentified woman walks down the far aisle, past the odd numbered stations, and into the heart of the small crowd; directly up to a woman dressed in a long sleeve turtleneck blouse with matching but oversized bluejeans, making you think she either lost weight or is pretending to.

"Excuse me, I think I'm suppose't be here, I'm Marge Cumberlan. I called Mr. Lander earlier this week."

Reaching out a hand, "Pleased to meet you Marge, I'm Candy. Are you going to sing with us?"

"I hope to, but I, well, I might not be good enough."

"Nonsense," says Candy, gently squeezing her arm as if to reassure, "you'll do fine. We'll help you."

Rehearsals move along and in a few weeks the newest member is officially assigned to the ten-thirty crew. At first, she finds it quite gratifying as many take notice of the fresh addition and openly express praise. However, the novelty soon dissipates and Mrs. Cumberlan's fleeting fame rudely expires. She becomes convinced that she's just another cantor, nothing special or unique.

She arrives early this weekend, hoping to have a minute alone before the others come. As the prior nine o'clock assembly departs, she hastily maneuvers her way up to the microphones. Looking around and seeing no one of significance, she bends down, on hands and knees, and crawls beneath the piano.

Knowing that people typically follow patterns and that they have their comfort zones, this day would likely be no different. Mass begins and the singers take their usual positions, two on the left microphone, and two on the right. After the entrance song, the director fiddles with the system until he discovers the problem, a disconnected cord. Marge tries to withhold a mischievous expression.

Another week has passed and it's Sunday morning again. Mrs. Cumberlan is early; though before long, Candy appears. Candy places her music on the right stand as she routinely does.

"How are you, Marge?" she asks while adjusting the stand from waist high to shoulder level.

Marge observes a frown forming. "What's wrong, Candy?"

"There's grease all over this stand! It's all over my hands!"

"You better wash it off, honey, I'll cover for you." Candy doesn't return until the gospel reading.

Similar disturbances occur the following two weekends, yet the four member team keeps on. This week, however, the music director has quietly assigned someone to guard the cantor's area prior to and during the ten-thirty Liturgy. The persistent woman shows up beforehand, but this time she notices someone nearby. Mass goes well.

Later that day, at home, down the basement, the seemingly rejuvenated widow begins rummaging through a number of boxes marked "John," the name of her late husband. Marge overturns several and spills their contents onto the cool, gray, cemented floor. Discovering the cardboard container, she lunges at it, it lifts easily. She finds three shells inside.

Now it's Sunday already and Mrs. Cumberlan is wearing a new dress for the special occasion. A stunted, subdued horn sounds in the yard where Candy and two other song leaders are waiting. Marge had said she was having car problems, although her Ford Tempo is still warm from the recent trip to the grocery store.

She waves at them to come in.

Candy checks her watch, "I guess we've got a minute." They exit the car and walk to the house.

"Please come in," Mrs. Cumberlan hollers from the back bedroom.

They gather in the kitchen, Candy enters last. Mrs. Cumberlan comes out with the rifle raised. She pulls the trigger and the one in front falls back. The remaining two momentarily freeze while she readies the gun for another discharge. In the living room, another blast is heard and she repeats the loading procedure. Out the door a third sounds, as the neighbors muster, and Candy tumbles to the ground holding her leg, makeup streaming down her face.

The overly anxious singer reaches St. Anthony's just before the entrance song. A familiar Sunday morning calm envelops the simply furnished church, though, Mrs. Cumberlan's stomach affords some interesting sensations as it responds to her anxiety-ridden excitement. The director rises from the organ bench and meets her halfway. He gently squeezes her arm and whispers, "You're solo today, the others haven't showed." Mr. Lander softly describes some final strategies while the priest lines up in the gathering area. Echoes of screeching tires and slamming doors emerge from the nothingness, and red and white flashes compete along the walls to brighten the otherwise subdued worship area.

The soloist shoves the officer away. "But I'm the cantor, it's my debut." She holds her ground and remains at her post, by the left microphone. Two policemen clutch her arms and escort her out.

Today, Mrs. Cumberlan solitarily proclaims church hymns to her new assembly, in her new home, the sanitarium.

...Do Today!...

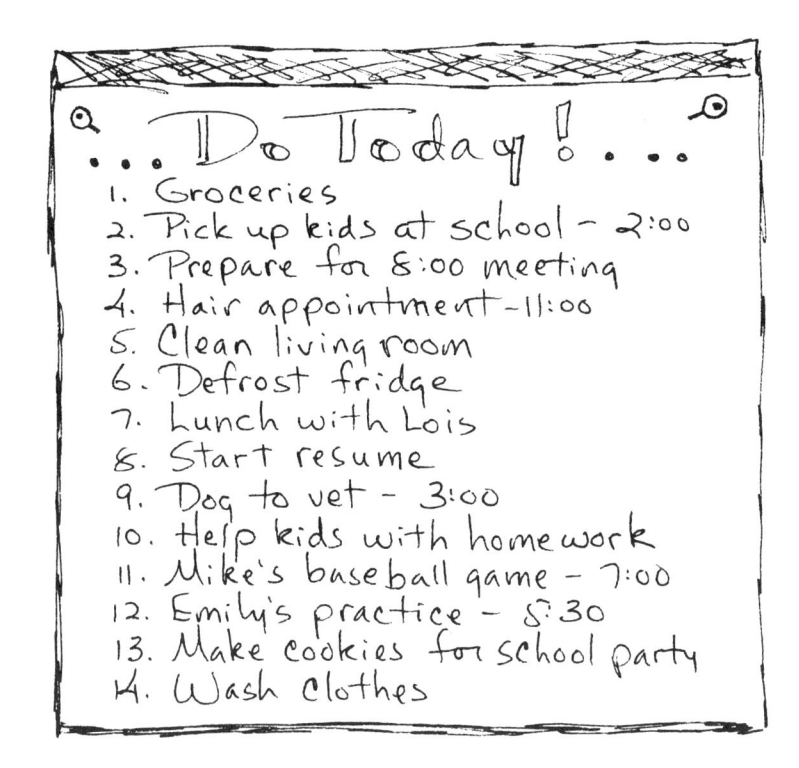

1. Groceries
2. Pick up kids at school - 2:00
3. Prepare for 8:00 meeting
4. Hair appointment - 11:00
5. Clean living room
6. Defrost fridge
7. Lunch with Lois
8. Start resume
9. Dog to vet - 3:00
10. Help kids with homework
11. Mike's baseball game - 7:00
12. Emily's practice - 8:30
13. Make cookies for school party
14. Wash clothes

A GOAL MAY CAUSE US TO FORGET LIFE'S MOST IMPORTANT PRIORITIES

when i allow myself
　　some
　　　　silence

　i allow myself

　to think
　　　to listen
　　　　to sense
　　　　　to feel

room for thought

Stony Man

Here we sit, just the two of us, in silence,
On cool, grey and white boulders the size of my car.
Out of safety's reach, small stones gather in reckless piles,
As if in conference; me wondering when they called their meeting
Or when they might call another.

At eye level, a hawk soars almost at arms length,
It searches the valley for substance while I fantasize a flight.
The uniformed one adjusts his scope, hoping for a peak at the nest.

The sun moves slowly, the breeze blows slightly,
The clouds descend, and peace seems real.
On Stony Man Mountain.

Taking time
for myself
is the only way
I maintain
this illusion of sanity

room for thought

THE ART OF LISTENING

BEGINS WITH OPENING ONE'S HEART TO ANOTHER'S DREAMS AND CONCERNS FOLLOWED BY

PAYING ATTENTION

THE TREASURE

In the corner of my dining room, between the faded couch and the wall, it lays motionless and without sound. Particles of dust have gathered upon its crest. I carefully slide it out from its waiting place, while being mindful to bend my knees. Grasping the handle firmly, I gently set it upon its side. Feelings of childhood return to me, a memory of unwrapping a much wanted Christmas gift, as I prepare to open this rock-like cocoon.

First I unlatch the middle clamp, followed by the left one, then the right. Why I detach the center one first is a mystery. Perhaps it is an unconscious ritual formed in the early days, some nine years ago. Like splitting the shell of an oyster to unveil a precious treasure, I open its black, rectangular hull.

I am greeted with the scent of something long abandoned and detained in storage. Everything from within appears just as I recall. The formula-treated cloth I use for caressing its smooth surface remains neatly folded in its designated sector with delicate strands of material sporadically hanging from its mass. My twin-pair of cords that aid to amplify otherwise muffled tones are still arranged in their figure eight formation, and the partially filled spray-can containing a lubricant which safeguards my fingertips from cuts is also present. I behold my most favored piece from within, besides the wooden beauty herself, the battery-driven tuner. With its red swinging pendulum, it guides my notes to pitch and shelters me against dissonance (those unsettling collisions of incompatible sounds).

I reach to release the ivory colored instrument from hibernation, using my left hand to grasp its silky, delicate neck. Feeling as the familiar embrace of an old and dear friend, I warmly fix it upon my shoulder, adjusting and unwinding the scaly textured strap. Unconsciously, I run my fingers over both ends, making certain the soft colored strap is firmly attached to the supporting bolts, thus preventing potential damage to my Fender if it should crash to the ground. Reaching again into my case, I raise the can of Finger-Ease and shake it well (the directions don't say to do this but I think it's a law: SHAKE ALL CANS WELL BEFORE USE!). I spray the strings.

    The guitar pick I choose today is my favorite, easily recognized by its bright red hue and its familiar placement between the Volume and the Tone controls. No longer are letters visible on its surface, but its linear design yields not to my pressures. I place my fingertips upon the fifth, sixth, and seventh frets, positioning them properly to form an A Major chord. Their cool, unfamiliar touch causes an awkwardness in my movements. Though lacking the grace of a practiced musician, I run my pick over these steel-threads (otherwise known as strings). Together, all six, make a piercing squeal similar to the results of car brakes long neglected, compel me to employ the talents of my tuner.

Behind
those eyes of yours
are
thoughts and feelings

I can't possibly understand

One of age
is a precious gift to the world

One of age
holds the knowledge of experience

One of age
One of age

what i might say

if i were to write about you
this is what i might say

to know you is to be unsure
                        of knowing you
to be forever searching
        for answers to new questions
to travel an endless highway
            with many
            winding patterns
            altering speed limits
            and
            confusing crossroads
to follow a mountain path
        high
        into the clouds
        where it embraces them
                    as friends
        and into
        a valley
        that it often calls its home

if i were to thank you
this is what i might say

for the morning
sweet splendor of morning

for the afternoon
life is in full bloom

for the evening
the serenity of evening

for the night
rest is welcomed

thank you

if I were to pray to you
this is what I might say

may I realize and use my gifts
        wisely
           and
                unselfishly

may I be true to my devotions
        and draw strength
      from them_____

may I be more like you
with each breath I take

      and I pray the same
      for all others

           whom could I dismiss

If you **LOVE** someone
SHOW IT

If you're **ANGRY** with someone
DEAL WITH IT

If you're **FOND** of someone
ENJOY IT

If you **DISLIKE** someone
GET OVER IT

If you're **PROUD** of someone
SAY IT

Your Song

You tell me I'm special, words not so easily heard.
You say to remember, my heart cry's out the thought.
Who are you?, this one, eye's just like mine.

Young in relations, sadness is knocking.
Could I understand what you're feeling?
That day at my wall, I get the news.
The white night has fallen, no words can make it better.

Then it was you, eyes stuck like glue.
Words don't come easy, words don't come at all.
Only the heart speaks through our eyes and touch.
If I could take your sadness, I can only offer you strength.

After the tears comes daylight, slowly but in time.
One does not replace another, only adds to the experience.
A new adventure to seek, a realized friendship to explore.
Risky as it is.

As once I had read, like attracts like.
Special you are to me, special you are to the earth.
Teacher are you, student are you, loved are you.

Come, let us walk.

finding begins with searching

searching
begins with trying

and
trying may begin by accident

my soul
is more hungry
than
my
mind

Inspiration flourishes
through
the observation of others

I often wonder though
what knowledge awaits birth
a gift only received
through attention to the self

like in a dream
separated
from this shell of mine
gliding
across, over, under, and above
carefully examining each color

what would be found
would I like it
should I change it
must I deny it
would I run in terror from it
do I love it

YES

I needed an opening line, you are it.

My friends often tell me I'm strong. Now, I don't believe this is in reference to the strength of a massively built Weight Lifter or a 500 pound Wrestler. They appear to be referring to my ability to handle everyday life's wonderfully, surprising, little challenges. You know, the one's we're all so fond of that are suppose to either make you stronger or kill you.

Personally, I find it annoying to be described as "strong." Don't you think that's an awful lot to live up to? Does this mean I always have to be strong? Can I breakdown once in a while, lose my temper, or maybe freak out briefly (claim temporary insanity)? Should I include this on my resume?

When it comes down to it, we're all strong in some respect. You, reading this, are alive. You've survived another day. Therefore, you must be strong. The old couple driving 30mph on the highway attempting to reach Sunday services on time, the driver clutching the wheel with both hands not quite sure which lane is really theirs, they are strong. And you, the one who always gets stuck behind them, you're strong.

We are all strong.

I needed a closing line, this is it.

Many of the sayings and illustrations in this book are available in the form of T-Shirts, posters, mugs and other items. Please complete the order form on the following page to receive our product catalog.

Order Form

Name: _____

Address: _____

City: _____ State: _____ Zip: _____

Phone: (____) _____

Quantity	Item	Unit Price	Total
	Things in Small Quantities Have Lasting Appeal	$12.95	
	Book Shipping and Handling	$3.00	
	Product Catalog *Cost Refunded with first purchase!*	$ 2.00	
	Catalog Shipping and Handling	*Free*	*Free*
		Grand Total	

Checks or money orders *(do not send cash)* payable to:

Academy Productions, Inc.
P.O. Box 19012
Cleveland OH   44119

Please allow 4-6 weeks for delivery.